Go For It, Charlie Brown

Charles M. Schulz

Selected cartoons from
DR. BEAGLE AND MR HYDE
Volume 3

CORONET BOOKS
Hodder and Stoughton

PEANUTS Comic Strips by Charles M. Schulz
Copyright © 1980, 1981 by United Feature Syndicate, Inc.

First published in the United States of America 1983 by
Ballantine Books
Coronet edition 1984

British Library C.I.P.

Schulz, Charles M.
  Go for it, Charlie Brown.
  I. Title
  741.5'973   PN6727.S3

  ISBN 0–340–34701–5

Printed and bound in Great Britain for
Hodder and Stoughton Paperbacks, a
division of Hodder and Stoughton Ltd.,
Mill Road, Dunton Green, Sevenoaks,
Kent (Editorial Office: 47 Bedford
Square, London, WC1 3DP) by
Cox & Wyman Ltd., Reading

**Also by the same author,
and available in Coronet Books:**

SEVEN, EIGHT, NINE, TEN! *HA!!*

"7+3=10"...THAT'S AN EASY ONE, MARCIE...

ANYTHING WITH A "3" IS EASY BECAUSE YOU JUST TAKE THE FIRST NUMBER AND THEN COUNT THE LITTLE POINTY THINGS ON THE "3," AND YOU HAVE THE ANSWER!

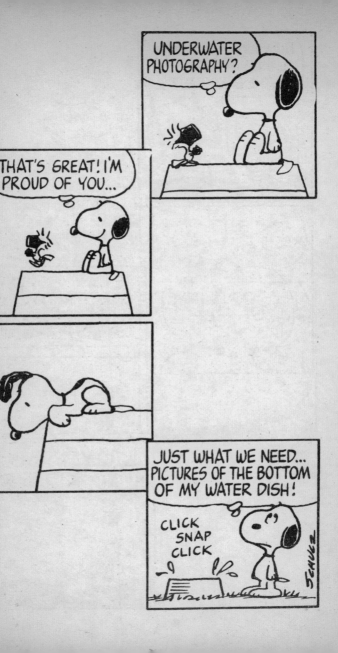

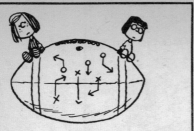

I THINK WE SHOULD PRACTICE SOMETHING DIFFERENT THIS TIME..

NOT TOO DIFFERENT, SIR...

THIS IS THE PLAY, MARCIE... YOU GO STRAIGHT OUT, CUT LEFT, CUT BACK, GO STRAIGHT, CUT BACK, GO RIGHT AND THEN OUT...

HAVE YOU GOT THAT?

I THINK SO, SIR..I GO OUT LEFT, CUT STRAIGHT, CUT RIGHT, CUT BACK, GO LEFT, CUT BACK, GO STRAIGHT, CUT LEFT AND RUN RIGHT...

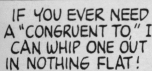

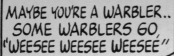

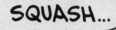

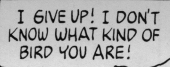
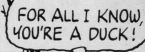

YES, MA'AM, I PICKED THEM MYSELF...AREN'T THEY BEAUTIFUL?

DO WE HAVE A VASE AROUND HERE?

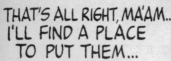

THAT'S ALL RIGHT, MA'AM.. I'LL FIND A PLACE TO PUT THEM...

Z

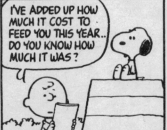

➡

BUT FIRST HE LOOKS OVER ALL THE PUMPKIN PATCHES TO SEE WHICH ONE IS THE MOST SINCERE..IF HE CHOOSES THIS PUMPKIN PATCH, I'LL GET TO MEET HIM!

THIS YEAR I JUST KNOW HE'S GOING TO CHOOSE THIS PUMPKIN PATCH!! I JUST KNOW IT!

OH, WHAT A GLORIOUS MOMENT THAT WILL BE!!!

SEE?

HOW SHARPER THAN A SERPENT'S TOOTH IS A SISTER'S "SEE?"

GETTING READY FOR BED CAN BE A REAL CHORE...

YOU SHOULD MAKE SURE YOUR BOOKS AND THINGS ARE SET PROPERLY FOR SCHOOL THE NEXT DAY...

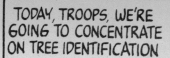

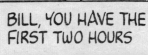

I HATE THE CHANGING OF THE GUARD!

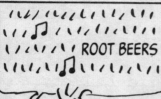

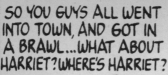

IN CASE YOU'RE WONDERING, HARRIET IS ALL RIGHT..THE ROUND-HEADED KID IS GOING TO BAIL HER OUT...

SO YOU SAY YOU WERE IN THIS PLACE CALLED "THE BIRDBATH" DRINKING ROOT BEER WHEN THESE BLUE JAYS CAME IN...

THEY STARTED TO GET INSULTING, AND THAT'S WHEN IT HAPPENED, HUH? THAT'S WHEN SHE DID IT?

THAT'S WHEN HARRIET HIT THE BLUE JAY IN THE FACE WITH THE ANGEL FOOD CAKE!

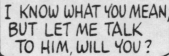

WELL, BIRD, I HATE TO SAY IT, BUT I DON'T HAVE ANY IDEA WHERE WE ARE...

I'M GETTING HUNGRY, TOO..

YOU KNOW WHAT WOULD TASTE GOOD RIGHT NOW? A BIG PIECE OF ANGEL FOOD CAKE!

"SEVEN MINUTE FROSTING"
2 UNBEATEN EGG WHITES
1½ CUPS SUGAR
5 TBSP. COLD WATER
⅛ TSP. SALT
⅛ TSP. CR. OF TA.

SCHULZ

MARCIE, CHUCK'S LOST IN THE WOODS..HE NEEDS US TO FIND HIM...

GET YOUR BACKPACK.. BRING ALL THE THINGS YOU NEED IN THE WOODS! WE'RE A RESCUE TEAM!!

I HAVE EVERYTHING, SIR.. FOOD, WATER AND COMIC BOOKS...

IT MAY BE A LONG TRIP...BRING AN EXTRA COMIC BOOK!

GOOD GRIEF, MARCIE, HOW DID YOU GET SO TALL?

IT'S MY EXPEDITION BOOTS, SIR..WHILE WE'RE LOOKING FOR CHUCK, WE MIGHT RUN INTO SOME BAD WEATHER...

THESE BOOTS ARE FILLED WITH GOOSE DOWN..

BUT DON'T WORRY, SIR.. IF WE MEET A GOOSE, YOU CAN PRETEND YOU DON'T KNOW ME!

YOU KNOW WHAT I THINK, LITTLE BIRD?

I THINK YOU SHOULD FLY OFF INTO THE AIR, AND TRY TO FIND SNOOPY BY YOURSELF...

TELL HIM I DID MY BEST! TELL HIM I'M LOST! TELL HIM I'M SORRY!

BETTER YET, JUST SAY, "RATS!" HE'LL UNDERSTAND!

YOU KNOW WHAT WE FORGOT, SIR? WE FORGOT TO BRING ALONG AN AUTOMATIC DUCK PLUCKER

IF WE DECIDE TO HAVE DUCK FOR DINNER, WE SHOULD HAVE AN AUTOMATIC DUCK PLUCKER

AN AUTOMATIC DUCK PLUCKER CAN PLUCK ONE DUCK IN EIGHTY SECONDS OR FIFTY-THREE DUCKS IN SIXTY MINUTES!

YOU DON'T SEEM INTERESTED, SIR...

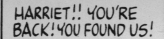

THE COMIC BOOKS ARE COMING LOOSE FROM MY FEET, MARCIE...PAGES ARE FLYING ALL OVER...

LET ME SEE WHAT I CAN DO...

DID YOU EVER READ THIS ONE, SIR? IT'S WHERE SPIDERPERSON IS ON THIS BRIDGE, AND...

MARCIE!

SORRY, SIR..

HOW'D YOU LIKE THAT RESCUE OPERATION, CHUCK? MARCIE AND I BRAVED A BLIZZARD TO FIND YOU AND YOUR DOG!

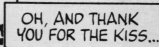

OH, AND THANK YOU FOR THE KISS...

KISS? I DIDN'T KISS ANYBODY..

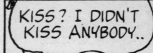

JUST CALL ME "SUGAR LIPS"

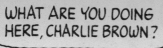

I'VE READ A LOT ABOUT ABRAHAM LINCOLN WHEN HE WAS AN ATTORNEY...

NOT ONCE, ON THE DAY OF A TRIAL, WAS HE UNABLE TO FIND THE COURTHOUSE

LIFE WAS SIMPLER THEN!

SCHULZ

➡

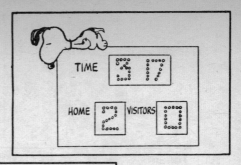

TODAY IS BEETHOVEN'S BIRTHDAY..HE WAS BORN IN BONN, IN 1770...

MY AUNT MARIAN ALWAYS USED TO SAY SHE WAS BORN IN BED SO SHE COULD BE NEAR HER MOTHER!

BONK!

IT WAS PROBABLY AN "IN" JOKE

"AND LAID HIM IN A MANGER BECAUSE THERE WAS NO ROOM FOR THEM IN THE INN..." LUKE 2:7

SOME SCHOLARS FEEL THAT THE "INN" MORE LIKELY WAS A PRIVATE HOME WITH A GUEST ROOM

"MANGER" COULD ALSO BE CONFUSING HERE SO SOME SCHOLARS THINK THAT PERHAPS THE...

WOULDN'T IT BE NEAT TO HAVE A CHRISTMAS TREE COMPLETELY COVERED WITH JUST CANDY CANES?

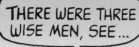

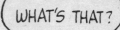

SOME OF THESE LEASH LAWS ARE RIDICULOUS!

IF YOU WANT SOMETHING DONE RIGHT, YOU SHOULD DO IT YOURSELF!

I'VE BEEN LOOKING FORWARD TO GOING OUT TONIGHT...

I MADE THE DINNER RESERVATIONS MYSELF, AND I EVEN BOUGHT A NEW BOW TIE...

BUT I NEVER SHOULD HAVE LET WOODSTOCK ORDER THE HATS!

"HANS BRINKER AND THE SILVER SKATES"... TWO HUNDRED AND THIRTY-SEVEN PAGES!

IF I READ ONE PAGE A DAY, MARCIE, I'LL BE DONE ON AUGUST TWENTY-THIRD

IF YOU HADN'T WASTED TIME FIGURING THAT OUT, SIR, YOU'D ALREADY BE ON PAGE TEN...

YOU'RE FUN TO BE AROUND, MARCIE

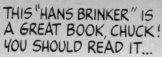

MORE SIDE-SPLITTING HUMOUR FROM PEANUTS AND CORONET

CHARLES M. SCHULZ

All these books are available at your local bookshop or newsagent, or can be ordered direct from the publisher. Just tick the titles you want and fill in the form below.

Prices and availability subject to change without notice.

CORONET BOOKS, P.O. Box 11, Falmouth, Cornwall.

Please send cheque or postal order, and allow the following for postage and packing:

U.K. – 45p for one book, plus 20p for the second book, and 14p for each additional book ordered up to a £1.63 maximum.

B.F.P.O. and EIRE – 45p for the first book, plus 20p for the second book, and 14p per copy for the next 7 books, 8p per book thereafter.

OTHER OVERSEAS CUSTOMERS – 75p for the first book, plus 21p per copy for each additional book.

Name ....

Address..

....